I0408920

# THE ART OF PROBLEM SOLVING

## Mastering the Skills to Overcome Any Challenge

Ray Goodwin

# CONTENTS

Title Page

Copyright

Liability Disclaimer

# LIABILITY DISCLAIMER

The information contained within this book is intended for informational purposes only and should not be construed as legal or professional advice. The authors and publishers of this book are not responsible for any losses or damages that may arise from the use of the information contained within.

The reader assumes full responsibility for any decisions made based on the information in this book. The authors and publishers do not endorse any particular method, service or product mentioned in this book and are not responsible for any consequences resulting from their use.

The reader should exercise caution and discretion when making life changing decisions, and should be aware of the risks and potential consequences of their actions. This book is not a substitute for professional or legal advice and should not be relied upon as such.

By reading and using the information in this book, the reader acknowledges and agrees to hold harmless the authors, publishers, and any other parties involved in the creation or distribution of this book from any and all liability, claims, damages, or losses that may arise from their use of the information contained herein.

# CHAPTER 1: INTRODUCTION TO PROBLEM SOLVING

Welcome to The Art of Problem Solving! This book is designed to help you tackle any challenge that comes your way. Whether it's a math problem, a business obstacle, or a personal dilemma, the skills and strategies in this book will empower you to find creative solutions.

I've spent my career working in diverse fields where problem solving was at the heart of every task. Through trial and error, I've discovered that there's an art to problem solving--a unique approach that combines logic, creativity, and intuition.

In this book, I'll share with you the principles of this art and provide practical exercises so you can develop your own problem-solving abilities. You'll learn how to break down complex problems into manageable pieces, how to brainstorm ideas effectively, and how to evaluate potential solutions to find the best one.

But more than just teaching techniques, this book will also inspire you on a deeper level. You'll discover stories of successful problem solvers from all walks of life who overcame obstacles through persistence and ingenuity. You'll be challenged to think differently about the problems you face and embrace them as opportunities for growth and learning.

So if you're ready to become a master problem solver and unlock your full potential, let's begin!

## Overview

Problem solving is an essential part of life. Every day, we encounter situations that require us to make decisions, find solutions, identify the best options, and take actions that will lead to successful outcomes. It is a process that involves critical thinking, creativity, and rationality. The ability to solve problems efficiently and effectively is a sought-after skill in many industries and professions, and it can be learned and developed by anyone.

## The Importance of Problem Solving Skills

The skill of problem solving is essential to success in the modern world. Many industries and professions reward individuals who can think critically and creatively, assess situations accurately, make effective decisions, take calculated risks, and communicate their ideas clearly to others. By developing problem solving skills, individuals can improve their productivity, creativity, and resourcefulness, thus enhancing their capacity to achieve both personal and professional goals. Problem solving skills are essential for career advancement, entrepreneurship, innovation, and creativity.

## Different Types of Problems

There are many different types of problems, ranging from simple and straightforward to complex and multifaceted. Some of the commonly encountered problems include mathematical problems, logical problems, analytical problems, social problems, technological problems, and personal problems. The type of problems faced, and their level of complexity, will affect the approach that needs to be taken to solve them.

## The Process of Problem Solving

The process of problem solving generally involves several key steps that need to be followed to achieve effective results. The steps include:

- ❖ Understanding and defining the problem
- ❖ Generating and evaluating possible solutions
- ❖ Choosing the best solutions
- ❖ Implementing the solutions
- ❖ Monitoring and evaluating the results
- ❖ Refining and improving the solutions

## Common Obstacles in Problem Solving

Despite its importance, problem solving can be challenging, and there are various obstacles that can get in the way of successfully solving a problem. Some of the most common obstacles include cognitive bias, lack of creativity, limited information, emotional interference, and poor communication.

## Benefits of Problem Solving

There are numerous benefits associated with being a good problem solver. Effective problem-solving skills can lead to increased productivity, improved outcomes, higher morale, and greater job satisfaction. Additionally, well-developed problem solving skills can help us to make better choices and avoid negative outcomes.

## Real-life Examples of Successful Problem Solvers

Many successful individuals attribute their success to their problem-solving skills. For instance, Elon Musk, the CEO of SpaceX and Tesla, has been able to solve complex problems and innovate within numerous established industries. Another example is Jeff Bezos, the founder and CEO of Amazon, who has been able to transform the way people shop online by offering innovative solutions to complex logistical problems.

## Overview of the Book

This book, The Art of Problem Solving, is designed to be a comprehensive guide to developing strong problem solving skills. It will explore the different types of problems people face and the various techniques used to solve them. The book aims to help individuals become more effective and efficient in solving problems, using logic, creativity, and critical thinking, and providing real-life examples of successful problem solving. The following chapters will take the reader through the steps of problem solving, from understanding the problem, brainstorming solutions, evaluating them to implementing solutions, and optimizing and improving the problem-solving process. Furthermore, the book will also explore different contexts for problem solving and address specific challenges and opportunities that people face in the digital age. Finally, the book concludes with a look at ethics and problem-solving, reviewing the importance of ethics in decision-making and leadership, and identifying potential ethical dilemmas that people may encounter when problem-solving. Throughout the book, readers will gain valuable insights, frameworks, methods, and tools for problem-solving, and learn how to apply these skills to both personal and professional contexts.

# CHAPTER 2: UNDERSTANDING THE PROBLEM

Any problem-solving process begins with a clear definition of the problem, which lays the foundation for brainstorming solutions and eventually implementing the best fit solution. The process of understanding the problem requires breaking down complex issues, exploring underlying assumptions, and analyzing the problem from multiple perspectives. Visualization is also a powerful tool for understanding problems, and this chapter will delve into this process, with real-life examples of problem understanding.

## The Importance of Clearly Defining the Problem

The first step to solving any problem effectively is gaining clarity on what the problem is. Without a clear definition, it becomes much harder to come up with effective solutions. Sometimes the problem we initially see is more of a symptom and not actually the root problem. Failing to address the underlying cause can mean that any solution will only be temporary, and the initial problem will continue to reoccur.

For example, imagine a bakery that is consistently receiving complaints about their bread being too hard. Upon closer inspection, it becomes clear that the oven temperature is out of sync, and the heat is fluctuating, resulting in overbaked bread that is difficult to eat. This knowledge will guide the baker to change the thermostat or implement a new oven to solve the root problem instead of adjusting the recipe, which will have only a temporary effect.

## Techniques for Breaking Down Complex Problems

Breaking down complex problems into manageable parts can help clarify tasks, highlights different angles, and help with decision making. One effective technique is to break down the problem according to its overarching categories and create sub-headings for each category. The subheadings will then become the focus of solution brainstorming. For instance, if the focus is on a new product, the categories may include marketing, production, gear, and employees.

## Identifying Assumptions

Unchallenged assumptions in a problem-solving situation can be a barrier to success. Identifying underlying assumptions is important because it allows us to question the validity of our perceptions, and that of others. After breaking down the complex problem, it is crucial to identify any underlying assumptions that could be clouding our perception so that we can decide whether they help or hinder the search for solutions.

## How to Ask the Right Questions

To solve a problem, one has to be curious and ask the right questions. Questions that start with 'why', what, 'when, 'where, and 'how' are useful for eliciting vital information for a problem. Questions that challenge assumptions, appeal to values, and incorporate all perspectives will ensure that creative and comprehensive solutions are generated.

## Analyzing the Problem from Different Perspectives

Solving some problems requires a shift in perspective that cannot be seen from one point of view. Looking at different angles can potentially reveal constraints or opportunities that would have gone unexplored. Take a situation where a business is struggling with decreasing sales; the problem may be an internal operational issue or a product deficiency or an external supply chain disruption. Each perspective reveals different responses to solve the problem. By viewing a problem from multiple viewpoints, individuals can gain a broader understanding of the issue they are trying to solve.

## Using Visualization to Understand the Problem

Visualization is a crucial part of understanding a problem, as it can highlight potential solutions that may go unnoticed by the logical mind. It helps to represent problems on paper visually. Mapping techniques such as spider diagrams, mind maps, and flowcharts make it possible to see the steps involved in the problem-solving process, the connections between problems and solutions, and the strategies necessary for resolving the problem.

## Real-Life Examples of Problem Understanding

Real-life examples of problem understanding provide insight into how different organizations approach problem-solving with an open mind. The comparison also highlights how companies that don't understand how to break down complex issues often have their goals on the wrong problem. For instance, when the United States Postal Service was losing an estimated $25 million per day, stakeholders saw the problem as missed opportunities to generate more revenue. After assessing, USPS officials discovered that cutting distribution services, such as mail sorting, and closing low-revenue post offices would save millions of dollars.

## Conclusion

The understanding of a problem is the bedrock of any successful problem-solving process. This chapter has examined several techniques for breaking down complex problems and ways to analyze the problem from different perspectives. Identifying assumptions and asking the right questions in analyzing the problem from multiple angles, can provide the clarity needed to select the best-fit solution. Techniques for using visualization have also been supplied, along with real-life examples of problem understanding. By developing a solid understanding of a problem, individuals and organizations are better equipped to find the right solution.

# CHAPTER 3: BRAINSTORMING SOLUTIONS

When faced with a problem, the most obvious thing to do is to find a solution. However, finding the right solution to a problem is rarely straightforward. It takes creativity, open-mindedness, and collaboration to brainstorm solutions that address the root cause of a problem. In this chapter, we will explore the art of brainstorming solutions.

**Techniques for Generating Ideas**

Brainstorming is a technique that involves generating as many ideas as possible, without judgment or criticism. The goal is to produce a large quantity of ideas, regardless of their quality. The purpose of this technique is to encourage creativity and to ensure that no possible solution is overlooked.

There are several techniques that can be used to generate ideas, such as mind mapping, word association, and random word generation. Mind mapping involves creating a visual representation of ideas, concepts, and thoughts related to the problem being solved. Word association involves thinking of words that are related to the problem and then using them as a starting point for generating ideas. Random word generation involves using a random word generator to generate words that can be used as inspiration for generating ideas.

## Importance of Quantity Over Quality

When brainstorming, it is important to focus on quantity over quality. This means that all ideas should be considered, regardless of how feasible or realistic they may be. A seemingly unrealistic idea may spark a more practical solution, or it could serve as a starting point for a more creative solution.

## Encouraging Creativity

Creativity is a key element of brainstorming. Encouraging creativity means being open to new ideas and approaches, without judgment or criticism. This can be achieved by creating a safe and supportive environment where team members feel comfortable sharing their ideas and opinions.

## The Role of Collaboration in Brainstorming

Brainstorming is often a collaborative process that involves bringing together people with different backgrounds and perspectives. Collaboration allows for a diversity of ideas and promotes a sense of ownership and commitment to the problem-solving process. It also ensures that all stakeholders are involved in the process.

## Evaluating Potential Solutions

The purpose of brainstorming is to generate as many ideas as possible, regardless of their quality. However, once all ideas have been generated, it is important to evaluate the potential solutions before refining them.

Evaluating potential solutions involves assessing each idea in terms of its feasibility, effectiveness, and potential for success. This requires considering the risks and benefits of each potential solution.

## Refining Solutions Through Iteration

Once potential solutions have been evaluated, the next step is to refine them. Refining involves dissecting the solutions and identifying specific steps that can be taken to improve them. This can involve modifying the solutions or combining ideas to create a better solution.

Refinement is an iterative process that requires testing and re-testing until the optimal solution is achieved.

## Real-Life Examples of Successful Brainstorming

Brainstorming has been used successfully in a variety of contexts to solve complex problems. In the pharmaceutical industry, for example, brainstorming sessions have been used to identify new drug targets and to develop new drugs. In the automotive industry, brainstorming sessions have been used to redesign production processes and to identify issues related to quality control.

In the healthcare industry, brainstorming sessions have been used to develop new treatments for diseases, to improve patient care, and to streamline administrative processes. In government agencies, brainstorming sessions have been used to identify new policies and procedures, to improve customer service, and to reduce costs.

## Conclusion

Brainstorming is a critical component of the problem-solving process. It allows for a diversity of ideas, promotes creativity and collaboration, and ensures that all stakeholders are involved in the process. By focusing on quantity over quality, encouraging creativity, and evaluating potential solutions, organizations can generate innovative solutions to complex problems.

Real-life examples demonstrate how brainstorming has been successfully used to solve problems across a variety of industries. The key takeaway is that brainstorming can be used in any setting to generate new ideas and to solve complex problems.

# CHAPTER 4: EVALUATING SOLUTIONS

After brainstorming solutions, it is important to evaluate them against certain criteria to determine which solution is best suited to solve the problem at hand. Evaluating solutions involves weighing the pros and cons of each option and considering possible trade-offs. In this chapter, we will discuss the criteria for evaluating solutions, the importance of considering trade-offs, and the different methods of quantitative and qualitative analysis.

## Criteria for Evaluating Solutions

When evaluating solutions, it is important to consider multiple criteria to ensure that the chosen solution meets the desired outcomes. The following are some criteria that can be used to evaluate solutions:

- ❖ Effectiveness: The solution must be effective in solving the problem without causing any new problems.

- ❖ Feasibility: The solution must be feasible in terms of cost, time, and resources.

- ❖ Scalability: The solution should be scalable and adaptable to different scenarios.

❖   Sustainability: The solution should be sustainable in terms of its impact on the environment, economy, and society.

❖   User Experience: The solution should take into account how users will interact with it and should be designed with their needs in mind.

❖   Ethics: The solution should be ethical and in line with the values of the organization.

## Considering Trade-offs

When evaluating solutions, it is important to consider possible trade-offs, as no solution is perfect. This involves weighing the benefits and drawbacks of each solution and choosing the one with the least negative consequences. For example, a solution may be effective but expensive, or it may be sustainable but not scalable. It is important to consider these factors and choose the solution that strikes the best balance between them.

## Quantitative and Qualitative Analysis

There are different methods of analysis that can be used to evaluate solutions. These can be broadly classified into quantitative and qualitative analysis.

Quantitative analysis involves using numerical data to evaluate solutions. This can be done through cost-benefit analysis, which involves weighing the costs and benefits of different solutions in monetary terms. For example, if the problem is a high employee turnover rate, the cost of recruiting and training new employees can be compared to the benefits gained through reduced turnover.

Another quantitative method is risk assessment, which involves identifying potential risks associated with each solution and evaluating the probability and severity of those risks. This can help organizations make informed decisions and take necessary precautions to mitigate risks.

Qualitative analysis involves using subjective data to evaluate solutions. One method is to use a decision matrix, which involves assigning weights to different criteria and evaluating solutions based on these weights. This can be a useful tool when there are multiple criteria to consider and can help organizations make more informed decisions.

## Real-life Examples of Successful Solution Evaluation

One example of successful solution evaluation comes from the healthcare industry. In 2012, a hospital in Boston, Massachusetts implemented a program to reduce patient readmissions. The hospital created a team of nurses, pharmacists, and social workers to provide follow-up care to patients after they were discharged from the hospital. The team worked with patients to ensure they understood their medication regimens and had access to any necessary resources.

After implementing the program, the hospital saw a 25% reduction in readmissions within 30 days of discharge. The program not only improved patient outcomes, but also saved the hospital an estimated $2 million in costs associated with readmissions.

Another example comes from the technology industry. In 2009, Apple introduced the iPhone 3GS, which included a number of new features, including voice control and faster processing speeds. The company evaluated the new features against criteria such as user experience and feasibility and found that the new features would significantly enhance the user experience while still being feasible in terms of cost and time. The decision to include these features helped Apple maintain its competitive edge in the smartphone market.

## Conclusion

Evaluating solutions is an important step in the problem-solving process. By considering the criteria for evaluating solutions and the possible trade-offs, organizations can make informed decisions and choose the solution that best meets their needs. Quantitative and qualitative analysis can also be used to evaluate solutions, and real-life examples demonstrate the importance of effective solution evaluation in achieving successful outcomes.

# CHAPTER 5: IMPLEMENTING SOLUTIONS

In the previous chapters, we have discussed the importance of understanding the problem, brainstorming solutions, and evaluating them. However, none of these steps can be effective unless the solutions are implemented. Implementing solutions is the stage where you convert your ideas into actions, and a successful implementation means your problem is solved. In this chapter, we will discuss how to implement the chosen solution effectively.

### Plan and execute a solution

Before implementing any solution, it is important to plan everything that needs to be done. The implementation plan should be based on the detailed evaluation of the solution. Once the plan has been developed, it should be executed precisely. Each step must be taken in the order specified, and deadlines must be set for each step. A plan is only as effective as its execution, so make sure you have a reliable team that follows the plan and can adapt to any changes that arise.

### Overcoming obstacles

No matter how great your plan is, obstacles will arise. Some of the obstacles could be external, such as regulatory or market changes, while others could be internal, such as employee resistance or insufficient funds. It is important to address these obstacles as soon as they arise. This includes anticipating obstacles that could arise and creating contingency plans. Identify potential problems and develop solutions before they become a problem, and make sure that resources are available to tackle any obstacle head-on without affecting the implementation process.

### The Importance of Monitoring Progress

Once the plan has been implemented, it is important to monitor progress to ensure that it is on track. This step is critical in ensuring that if issues arise in the implementation process, they can be addressed in real-time. Milestones should be identified in advance, and the progress should be tracked against the milestones that have been set. Regular team meetings, reports and updates based on the milestones will enable the team to review and adjust the plan where necessary and to take corrective action in a timely manner.

### Adjusting Course as Needed

Sometimes, even the best implementation plan can be derailed or delayed by unforeseen circumstances. It is important to monitor progress closely and identify the signs of things going wrong. If a problem arises and threatens the entire project, it is better to adjust the course and make modifications to the plan. One important point to remember is that the plan is a guide and not a rigid process. Hence, it should be adjusted if the situation warrants it. Adjusting the plan requires the team to work collaboratively and communicate with one another about potential issues arising and possible solutions.

### Leveraging Resources Effectively

Resources are required to implement a solution, including equipment, individuals, or funding. It is important to use the resources effectively to ensure that the solution is implemented successfully. The team must allocate resources to each activity based on the needs of that activity. It should be ensured that the resources are used optimally and not wasted, resulting in delays or the failure of implementation. Proper allocation of resources can make the difference between success and failure.

## Managing Stakeholders

Stakeholders play a vital role in any solution that is being implemented. They might include internal stakeholders such as employees or external stakeholders, which might include clients or regulatory agencies. It is important to manage stakeholders effectively to ensure that they receive updates and can provide feedback throughout the implementation process. Managing stakeholder expectations requires effective communication and collaboration throughout the process. Checking in with stakeholders to provide updates, ask for feedback, and address their concerns can help the implementation process move smoothly and may also help to build lasting relationships with them.

## Real-life examples of successful solution implementation

The implementation of any solution is challenging. Success stories can sometimes provide more insights than any theoretical explanation. Real-life examples of the solution implementation process include Steve Jobs' return to Apple in 1997 and the implementation of the One-Million Cataract Surgeries campaign in India. Steve Jobs returned to a struggling Apple and implemented a series of strategies that changed the fortunes of the company. In India, the One-Million Cataract Surgeries campaign was implemented by the Indian government and helped to eradicate blindness as a result of cataracts. Both of these examples show how the implementation process should be followed diligently and occasionally modified to accommodate situations. These examples also prove that successful implementation requires a strategic plan and the ability to adapt to challenges that arise during the implementation stages.

## Conclusion

Implementing a solution is the most crucial step in problem solving. A well-planned and executed implementation process can lead to the successful resolution of the problem. Organizing the steps, planning, monitoring progress, adjusting plans, leveraging resources effectively, managing stakeholders and implementing the solution are the essential components of implementing a solution. Finally, when problems are resolved, it is important to reflect on the process and identify areas of improvement for future problem-solving.

# CHAPTER 6: REFLECTION AND OPTIMIZATION

Problem-solving is not a one-time event but rather a continuous process. To further improve one's problem-solving skills, it is vital to reflect on completed projects or solved problems and identify areas for improvement. Reflection provides an opportunity to evaluate the entire process and make adjustments where necessary.

**Importance of Reflecting on the Problem-Solving Process**

When one takes the time to reflect on a problem-solving process, it enables him or her to learn from successes and failures. Failure is not always a negative outcome because, through it, one can identify what went wrong and improve on it in future projects. Reflecting on successful projects can help one identify and strengthen areas that contributed to the success.

Furthermore, reflection helps identify any systematic issues in the organization that may be hindering a successful problem-solving process. It helps to ensure that solutions don't need constant rework, and every problem-solving process becomes more precise and efficient.

**Identifying Areas for Improvement**

After reflecting on the process, it is essential to identify specific areas that need improvement. One should develop certain questions to ask such as; what could have been improved? Were all possible solutions explored? Was the data analyzed correctly? Once the problem areas have been identified, it's essential to develop realistic strategies for improvement.

## Celebrating Successes

Reflecting on one's problem-solving skills isn't just about identifying areas that need improvement. It's vital also to recognize and celebrate successes. It's not often that problems are solved, or projects completed successfully, and it takes diligence, hard work, and collaboration to achieve this, and it's always worth recognizing such successes. Celebrating successes, whether big or small, motivates one to keep using their problem-solving skills and enhances confidence.

## Strategies for Continuous Improvement

Continuous improvement strategies are focused on enhancing processes to make them more efficient, effective, and adaptive. Continuously updating problem-solving methods creates a culture of improvement, empowering oneself and the team to continuously innovate in problem-solving. These strategies entail the development of metrics to monitor the improvement efforts' progress and make necessary adjustments to reach one's goals.

## Real-life examples of successful reflection and optimization

Simon Sinek, a leadership expert, emphasizes reflective practices by daily taking at least five minutes to think about potential improvements and identifying opportunities for growth. Through reflective practices, Simon can identify areas where he might have missed something in the past and identify possible strategies for future improvement.

Another example is Taco Bell, a fast-food chain, which implemented a continuous improvement program which prompted employees to come up with creative ideas for improving the company's processes, and they were rewarded for any implemented ideas. This program led to their food-sales being produced 20% quicker from idea to implementation.

In conclusion, reflecting and optimizing on the problem-solving process is an integral part of improving one's skills. It assists in the identification of areas for improvement, celebration of successes, and development of strategies for continuous improvement. The problem-solving journey is a continuous one, and by embracing reflections and optimization, one can build better problem-solving skills over time.

# CHAPTER 7:
# STRATEGIC THINKING

Problem solving is an essential skill in today's rapidly changing business environment. Organizations must continually adapt to ensure that they remain competitive, relevant, and successful. To achieve this goal, strategic thinking is a critical component of problem solving. Strategic thinking involves identifying and defining strategic goals, developing a strategic plan, and anticipating potential risks and obstacles. In this chapter, we will explore the role of strategic thinking in problem solving and provide real-life examples of successful strategic thinking.

## Defining Strategic Goals

Strategic goals are long-term, high-level objectives that guide an organization's decision-making process. These goals help organizations stay focused on their core purpose, values, and mission. When defining strategic goals, it is essential to consider both internal and external factors that can impact the organization's success.

For example, if an organization is experiencing a decline in sales, its strategic goal may be to increase revenue. To achieve this goal, the organization may need to invest in new products, improve its marketing strategy, or expand its sales team. By identifying a clear and measurable strategic goal, the organization can ensure that all its efforts are aligned towards the same objective.

## Developing a Strategic Plan

Once strategic goals have been defined, the next step is to develop a strategic plan. A strategic plan outlines the steps that an organization will take to achieve its strategic goals. It includes detailed timelines, budgets, and the roles and responsibilities of the employees involved in the project. The strategic plan must be flexible enough to accommodate changes in the marketplace and internal factors.

For instance, if an organization's strategic goal is to launch a new product, the strategic plan may include developing a product roadmap, defining the pricing strategy, and conducting market research to identify potential customers. The plan must account for the potential challenges that the company may face and outline contingency plans to address those challenges.

## Identifying Potential Risks and Obstacles

No matter how well-defined the strategic goal and strategic plan, there will always be risks and obstacles to overcome. Therefore, identifying potential risks and obstacles is a crucial part of strategic thinking. By anticipating these challenges ahead of time, an organization can develop effective strategies to mitigate or overcome them.

For example, a software development company may have a strategic goal to launch a new software product. However, the development team may identify potential technical challenges that could delay the launch. To overcome this obstacle, the organization may allocate additional resources to the project or explore alternative solutions to the technical challenges.

## Importance of Flexibility in Strategic Planning

While having a well-defined strategic plan is essential, it is equally important to recognize the need for flexibility. Markets, consumers, and competitors are constantly changing, and strategic plans must accommodate these changes. Therefore, organizations must be prepared to adapt and adjust their plans to ensure that they remain relevant and competitive.

For example, a retail company may have a strategic goal to increase sales by launching a new product line. However, it may realize that consumers are no longer interested in that product category and instead demand other types of products. To remain competitive, the company must be willing to adjust its strategic plan and develop new products that meet the changing demands of its customers.

## Real-life Examples of Successful Strategic Thinking

A compelling real-life example of successful strategic thinking is Apple Inc. Steve Jobs, the co-founder of Apple, was a master of strategic thinking. He was able to identify opportunities for growth in the market and develop innovative products that captured consumers' imaginations. One of Jobs' most significant strategic decisions was to develop the iPod, which revolutionized the music industry.

Jobs recognized that the music industry was shifting from physical media to digital downloads. He also observed that existing digital media players were bulky and unintuitive to use. To address these problems, Jobs developed the iPod, which was small, sleek, and easy to use. The iPod became a massive success and transformed the music industry. This example highlights how strategic thinking can identify opportunities for growth and offer innovative solutions to address market demand.

Another example of successful strategic thinking is Netflix. Netflix started as a DVD rental company but faced significant competition from other rental companies like Blockbuster. However, the organization recognized the shift towards streaming video and invested in developing a streaming platform that is now ubiquitous. Netflix disrupted the industry by creating on-demand content that was not limited to physical media. Netflix's strategic thinking was essential for its success.

## Conclusion

Strategic thinking is a critical component of problem-solving. Identifying and defining strategic goals, developing a strategic plan, and anticipating potential risks and obstacles are essential skills for organizations to remain competitive and successful. Flexibility in strategic planning and the ability to adjust to the changing marketplace is vital in problem-solving. Real-life examples of successful strategic thinking, such as Apple and Netflix, can inspire organizations to take risks, identify opportunities for growth and, most importantly, overcome changes in the market and internal hurdles.

# CHAPTER 8: CRITICAL THINKING

Critical thinking is one of the most important skills for problem solving. It involves a systematic approach to analyzing information, evaluating evidence, and making decisions based on sound reasoning. In this chapter, we will discuss the importance of critical thinking in problem solving, explore strategies for identifying and assessing assumptions, and offer tips for avoiding cognitive biases.

## The Importance of Critical Thinking

Critical thinking is essential for effective problem solving because it helps us to identify and evaluate assumptions and evidence. Assumptions are the underlying beliefs that influence our thinking and decision making, and they can often be unconscious or taken for granted. By bringing these assumptions to the surface and analyzing them critically, we are better able to make informed decisions and develop more effective solutions.

Evaluating evidence is also an important part of critical thinking. Evidence can come in many forms, such as data, research studies, expert opinions, or personal experiences. Evaluating evidence involves assessing its quality, accuracy, relevance, and reliability. By critically evaluating evidence, we can ensure that our decisions are based on the most accurate and reliable information available.

## Identifying and Assessing Assumptions

One of the key aspects of critical thinking is the ability to identify and assess assumptions. This involves recognizing the beliefs and biases that underlie our thinking and decision making. There are several strategies that can help us to identify and assess assumptions:

❖ Challenge assumptions – One way to identify assumptions is to actively challenge them. Ask questions like "Why do we believe this is true?", or "What evidence do we have to support this assumption?" By questioning assumptions, we can gain a deeper understanding of the problem and develop more effective solutions.

❖ Use different perspectives – Another way to identify assumptions is to look at the problem from different perspectives. Consider how different people or stakeholders might view the problem, and how their beliefs and biases might influence their thinking. By understanding these different perspectives, we can broaden our thinking and develop more effective solutions.

❖ Reflect on personal biases – We all have personal biases that can influence our thinking and decision making. Reflect on your own biases and consider how they might be affecting your thinking. Are you making assumptions based on personal experience or limited data? By recognizing and addressing our personal biases, we can make more informed decisions and develop better solutions.

## Logical Reasoning

In addition to identifying and assessing assumptions, critical thinking also involves logical reasoning. Logical reasoning is the process of using evidence and reasoning to reach a conclusion or make a decision. There are several strategies that can help us to use logical reasoning effectively:

❖ Use deductive and inductive reasoning – Deductive

reasoning involves using general principles or rules to make specific conclusions, while inductive reasoning involves using specific observations or evidence to make general conclusions. By using both deductive and inductive reasoning, we can develop more complex and nuanced solutions.

❖   Evaluate arguments – To effectively use logical reasoning, we need to be able to evaluate arguments. This involves identifying the premises or evidence used to support the argument and evaluating the strength of the argument based on the quality of the evidence and the relevance of the premises.

❖   Connect evidence and conclusions – Finally, critical thinking involves connecting evidence and conclusions. This means identifying the evidence or data that supports our conclusions and ensuring that our reasoning is consistent with the evidence. By connecting evidence and conclusions, we can ensure that our decisions are based on sound reasoning and reliable evidence.

## Evaluating Evidence

Another important aspect of critical thinking is evaluating evidence. We are often presented with a variety of data, research studies, expert opinions, or personal experiences when trying to solve a problem. Evaluating evidence involves assessing its quality, accuracy, relevance, and reliability. There are several strategies that can help us to evaluate evidence effectively:

❖   Identify the source – One of the first steps in evaluating evidence is to identify the source. Consider the credibility and expertise of the source, and how it might affect the reliability of the evidence presented. Does the source have a vested interest in the outcome?

❖   Examine the methodology – The methodology used to

collect and analyze the data can also affect the reliability of the evidence. Consider the sample size, the sampling method, and the statistical significance of the findings. Is the evidence based on a single study, or has it been replicated in other studies?

❖ Evaluate the conclusions – Finally, critical thinking involves evaluating the conclusions drawn from the evidence. Are the conclusions consistent with the evidence presented? Is there evidence that contradicts the conclusions? By evaluating evidence critically, we can ensure that our decisions are based on reliable and accurate information.

## Avoiding Cognitive Biases

One of the biggest challenges in critical thinking is avoiding cognitive biases. Cognitive biases are the unconscious mental shortcuts that can influence our thinking and decision making. There are several common cognitive biases that can affect critical thinking, including:

❖ Confirmation bias – Confirmation bias is the tendency to seek out information that confirms our existing beliefs, and to ignore information that contradicts those beliefs. To avoid confirmation bias, we need to actively seek out evidence that challenges our assumptions and beliefs.

❖ Availability bias – Availability bias is the tendency to rely on the information that is most readily available, rather than considering all available evidence. To avoid availability bias, we need to actively seek out different sources of information and consider all available evidence.

❖ Anchoring bias – Anchoring bias is the tendency to rely too heavily on an initial piece of information when making decisions. To avoid anchoring bias, we need to consider multiple sources of information and evaluate each piece of evidence on its own merits.

By being aware of these biases, we can take steps to avoid them and make more informed and effective decisions.

**Real-life Examples of Critical Thinking in Action**

There are many examples of critical thinking in action, both in personal and professional contexts. For example, a doctor might use critical thinking to diagnose a patient's illness by analyzing symptoms, evaluating different treatment options, and considering the patient's individual circumstances. A business leader might use critical thinking to evaluate a complex problem, bring together multiple perspectives and stakeholders, and develop a comprehensive solution that takes into account the long-term consequences.

**Conclusion**

Critical thinking is an essential skill for problem solving. By identifying and assessing assumptions, using logical reasoning, evaluating evidence, and avoiding cognitive biases, we can make more informed and effective decisions. There are many real-life examples of critical thinking in action, and by developing our critical thinking skills, we can become more effective problem solvers in both our personal and professional lives.

# CHAPTER 9:
# ANALYTICAL THINKING

Analytical thinking is the ability to break down complex problems into smaller, more manageable components, analyze data and information objectively, and identify patterns and trends. Analytical thinking is an important part of problem solving as it enables the problem solver to gain a deeper understanding of the problem at hand and identify potential solutions that may not be immediately obvious.

**Methods for Analyzing Data and Information**

Analyzing data and information is an important part of analytical thinking. There are a number of methods that can be used to analyze data and information:

❖ Statistical Analysis: This involves using statistical methods to analyze data and identify patterns and trends. Statistical analysis can be used to identify correlations and make predictions based on the data.

❖ Root Cause Analysis: This involves identifying the underlying cause of a problem by analyzing the contributing factors. This method is often used in manufacturing and production to identify the cause of defects in products.

❖ Cost-Benefit Analysis: This involves weighing the costs

of a decision or solution against the benefits to determine whether it is worth pursuing. Cost-benefit analysis is often used in business to evaluate the potential return on investment of a project.

❖　　SWOT Analysis: This involves analyzing the strengths, weaknesses, opportunities, and threats of a situation or organization. SWOT analysis is often used in strategic planning to identify potential risks and opportunities.

## Importance of Objectivity in Analysis

Objectivity is an important aspect of analytical thinking. Objectivity enables the problem solver to analyze data and information objectively, without being influenced by personal biases or beliefs. Objectivity is particularly important when making data-driven decisions, as personal biases can lead to inaccurate analyses and flawed decision-making.

## Identifying Patterns and Trends

Identifying patterns and trends is an important part of analytical thinking. Patterns and trends can provide valuable insights into the underlying causes of a problem and can help to identify potential solutions. There are a number of methods that can be used to identify patterns and trends:

❖　　Data Visualization: This involves presenting data in a visual format, such as a graph or chart. Data visualization can help to identify patterns and trends that may not be immediately apparent when looking at raw data.

❖　　　Regression Analysis: This involves analyzing the relationship between two variables to identify patterns or trends. Regression analysis can be used to make predictions based on the data.

❖ Time-Series Analysis: This involves analyzing data over time to identify trends. Time-series analysis is often used in finance to identify trends in stock prices or other financial indicators.

## Using Tools for Data Analysis

There are a number of tools that can be used to analyze data and information. These tools can help to streamline the analytical process and make it more efficient. Some of the most commonly used data analysis tools include:

❖ Spreadsheet Software: Spreadsheet software, such as Microsoft Excel, can be used to manage and analyze large amounts of data. Spreadsheet software can perform calculations, create graphs and charts, and analyze data using statistical methods.

❖ Data Analysis Software: There are a number of software programs specifically designed for data analysis, such as SAS and SPSS. These programs can perform complex analyses and generate detailed reports.

❖ Business Intelligence Software: Business intelligence software, such as Tableau and Power BI, can be used to analyze data in real time and generate interactive reports.

## Importance of Communicating Results Effectively

Communicating results effectively is an important part of the analytical thinking process. Effective communication ensures that the results of the analysis are understood by all stakeholders and can be used to inform decision-making. There are a number of strategies that can be used to communicate results effectively, including:

❖ Using Visuals: Using charts, graphs, and other visuals can help to communicate complex data and information more effectively.

❖ Clear and Concise Language: Using clear and concise language can help to ensure that the results of the analysis are understood by all stakeholders.

❖ Tailoring the Message: Tailoring the message to the target audience can help to ensure that the results of the analysis are relevant and meaningful to the stakeholders.

## Real-life Examples of Analytical Thinking in Action

Analytical thinking is an essential part of problem solving and has been used to address a wide range of complex problems. Here are a few real-life examples of analytical thinking in action:

❖ Predictive Analytics in Healthcare: Predictive analytics has been used in healthcare to identify patients who are at high risk of developing complications or being readmitted to the hospital. By analyzing patient data, healthcare providers can identify patterns and trends that can be used to provide targeted interventions and improve patient outcomes.

❖ Supply Chain Optimization: Analytical thinking has been used in supply chain management to optimize inventory levels and reduce costs. By analyzing historical sales data and demand patterns, companies can identify trends and adjust inventory levels to ensure that they have enough products to meet demand without holding excess inventory.

❖ Fraud Detection in Banking: Analytical thinking has been used in banking to detect fraudulent activity. By analyzing transaction data, banks can identify patterns and behaviors that are indicative of fraud and take action to prevent losses.

In conclusion, analytical thinking is an essential part of problem solving. By breaking down complex problems into smaller components, analyzing data and information objectively, and identifying patterns and trends, problem solvers can gain a deeper understanding of the problem at hand and identify potential solutions. The use of tools and software can help to streamline the analytical process and make it more efficient. Effective communication of results is essential to ensure that the results of the analysis are understood by all stakeholders and can be used to inform decision-making.

# CHAPTER 10: CREATIVE THINKING

Creative thinking is an essential element in problem solving. This chapter focuses on techniques to promote creative thinking, that is, the generation of new and original ideas. The process of creative thinking often involves divergent thinking, which is the ability to think of many ideas in response to a single question or problem. Divergent thinking is different from convergent thinking, which is the ability to come up with a single, correct answer.

In problem solving, creative thinking involves generating lots of new ideas, even if some seem outlandish or impossible. Creative thinking is the spark that ignites innovation and is the foundation of the scientific method. Many successful entrepreneurs and inventors rely on their creative thinking skills to come up with new and innovative products. The following are some techniques to promote creative thinking:

## 1. Brainstorming

Brainstorming is a powerful tool for generating ideas. It can be done alone or in a group. The process involves setting a time limit, say 10-15 minutes, and writing down as many ideas as possible on a particular topic or problem. The key is quantity not quality, at this stage. Once all ideas have been exhausted, the group can review, discuss, and select the most promising ones.

## 2. Mind Mapping

Mind mapping is a visual way of generating ideas. It can be done using a piece of paper or a computer program. Start by writing the problem or challenge in the center and then adding branches that represent subtopics or related ideas. From each subtopic, add more branches with related ideas. The process continues until a set of ideas are generated.

## 3. Role-playing

Role-playing is a technique that allows individuals to see things from different perspectives. This technique involves acting out a scenario to help generate new ideas. One individual can play the role of a customer, while others can play the roles of employees or managers. The goal is to understand the needs and wants of the customer and then brainstorm potential solutions.

## 4. Random Word Association

Random word association is a technique that involves generating random words and then trying to relate them to the problem or challenge at hand. For example, if the problem is how to reduce waste in a manufacturing plant, generate a list of random words such as airplane, cloud, garden, and shoe. Then try to relate each word to the problem and generate new ideas.

## 5. Reverse Thinking

Reverse thinking involves turning the problem around and thinking about it in reverse. For example, instead of asking, "How can we increase revenue?" ask "How can we decrease revenue?" This technique can help individuals break out of their usual way of thinking and approach the problem from a different angle.

## 6. Free-writing

Free-writing entails writing down all ideas that come to mind without worrying about grammar or logical organization. The goal is to generate as many ideas as possible in a short amount of time. Once ideas are generated, review them and see which are feasible and useful.

## 7. Mindful observation

Mindful observation involves observing the problem or challenge without judgement. It could be achieved through taking a walk or engaging in activities such as drawing or painting. This technique helps to gain a fresh and new perspective on the problem.

In conclusion, creative thinking is important in problem-solving. By leveraging techniques such as brainstorming, role-playing, and free-writing, individuals can generate many creative ideas for potential solutions. The key is not to hold back and to generate as many ideas as possible. The next step is evaluating and selecting the most promising ideas.

# CHAPTER 11:
# DECISION MAKING

At some point in our lives, everyone has to make crucial decisions. Sometimes, the options we have to choose from are incredibly complicated, and we don't know which way to go. In such cases, making a decision becomes a challenge that requires special skills. In this chapter, we will learn the process of decision-making, the different factors that affect decisions, and how we can make the most effective decisions with the least risk.

## Process of Decision-Making

The decision-making process is quite elaborate and requires strict adherence to the steps involved. The first step of decision making is to identify the problem or opportunity. This involves understanding what the situation is, what problems it poses, and what opportunities are available to seize it. It is impossible to make the right decision without identifying the problem accurately.

Once you have identified the problem and opportunities, the next step of decision-making is determining the criteria for decision-making. Deciding criteria will require determining the critical factors and attributes that you will use to evaluate the different options you have. Be sure to identify criteria that are quantifiable, results-oriented, and applicable to the problem you are trying to solve.

The next step of the decision-making process is to assess the value of each option in relation to the criteria for decision-making. One of the best ways to do this is by creating a table where you list the different options you have and the different criteria you identified in step 2. You can then give a score to each option on each criterion, grading them on a scale of 1-10.

Once you have determined the value of each option, it is time to choose one. Remember that choosing the option should be based on the results obtained from valuating the option, the criteria, and the risk assessment. Have at least three of the best options and make a pros and cons list to evaluate how each of them matches the decision criteria before choosing the most effective option.

**Factors that Affect Decision-Making**

When making decisions, there are several factors that can affect decision-making. The first of these is emotional attachment. Emotional attachments can cloud a person's judgment, rendering it less effective. It is vital to make objective decisions and separate emotions from the decision-making process.

The second factor that affects decision-making is cognitive biases. Cognitive biases are the underlying assumptions and beliefs that individuals have, which can lead to incorrect perceptions and judgments. Examples of common cognitive biases include confirmation bias, where we only look for evidence that confirms our beliefs; the sunk cost fallacy, where we continue investing in a project even when it is apparent that it won't work; and the halo effect, where we make overall judgments about people or things based on our judgments of their attributes.

The third factor that affects decision-making is stress. The higher the pressure you feel when making decisions, the more likely you will make mistakes that could be costly. Remain calm and be confident when making decisions.

The fourth factor that affects decision-making is the availability of information. It is essential to have as much relevant information as possible to make the best decision. Always be thorough in your research and data analysis to ensure that the information you have is sufficient and valid.

The fifth factor that affects decision-making is the environment in which decisions are made. The environment must be conducive to good decision-making. It is also essential to have the right team in place to make effective decisions.

## Effective Decision Making

Effective decision-making requires both analytical thinking and creative thinking. Analytical thinking involves using logic and critical thinking to determine the pros and cons of each option. It involves breaking down complex information into smaller, more manageable pieces.

Creative thinking, on the other hand, involves creating new options and alternatives. This involves stepping outside the box and adopting a different perspective. It is essential to use both analytical and creative thinking when making decisions to generate the best possible outcomes.

Lastly, when making decisions, it is essential to consider the long-term consequences of each option. Always weigh the short-term gains or losses against the potential long-term gains or losses. Also, remember that there is no perfect decision, but some choices are more effective than others.

## Conclusion

Effective decision-making is critical in any situation. It is essential to follow a thorough and logical process that takes into account all the options and the consequences of each decision. Making decisions is about weighing the risks and benefits, balancing emotions with data, and choosing the most effective option for the long-term. By using analytical and creative thinking and considering all relevant information, you can make effective decisions that will help you succeed in your personal and professional life.

# CHAPTER 12:
# COLLABORATION

Collaboration is an essential aspect of problem-solving, and it involves working with others to achieve a common goal. When it comes to addressing complex problems, collaboration can bring together different skills, knowledge, perspectives, and experiences to generate innovative solutions. However, effective collaboration requires communication, trust, and a willingness to listen and consider different viewpoints. In this chapter, we will explore the benefits and challenges of collaboration, strategies for effective collaboration in problem-solving, the importance of communication, and how to manage conflict in collaboration.

**Benefits and Challenges of Collaboration**

Collaboration has a myriad of advantages in problem-solving. One of the primary benefits is the emergence of diverse knowledge and perspectives that team members bring to the table. By collaborating with others, you can explore a variety of approaches to solve the problem. Collaboration can also lead to greater brainstorming of ideas and solutions since different people often have their unique ways of approaching a problem.

However, collaboration can also be challenging. People may have conflicting personalities or ideas. They may not trust each other or operate with different personal preferences. Additionally, language barriers, cultural differences, and time constraints can also hinder effective collaboration.

## Strategies for Effective Collaboration in Problem Solving

To achieve effective collaboration in problem-solving, several strategies should be considered, these include:

* ❖ Identify Roles and Responsibilities: Be clear about everyone's roles and responsibilities so that they know what they are accountable for and contribute to the best of their abilities.

* ❖ Develop a Shared Understanding of the Problem: Collaborators should have a shared understanding of the problem they are trying to solve. Understanding must include knowing the problem scope, history, and possible solutions.

* ❖ Encourage Active Listening: Actively listening to others helps individuals in a group to understand other viewpoints. It can create an environment of trust where other team members feel comfortable sharing their opinions. By paying attention to the underlying meaning of what someone is saying, you can better understand their perspective.

* ❖ Embrace Diversity: To maximize the benefits of collaboration, it is essential to embrace diversity. Acknowledging different strengths, skills, and backgrounds of colleagues can help teams create more innovative solutions.

* ❖ Set Deadlines and Prioritize Tasks: Setting realistic deadlines and prioritizing tasks can assist in meeting the project timeline, monitoring progress, and making adjustments, as necessary.

## Importance of Communication in Collaboration

Communication is vital in every aspect of collaboration. Effective communication allows team members to stay informed about project progression, updates, and changes in requirements. Participants need to feel comfortable sharing their thoughts and ideas and be able to offer constructive criticisms when needed. Good communications help everyone get a robust idea of team processes, who is responsible for what, and general expectations.

## Managing Conflict in Collaboration

As with most collaborative efforts, conflicts are likely to arise. Conflicts are not necessarily bad. They only become a problem if they are not managed properly, leading to unresolved issues, and stifling innovation. Conflicts may arise due to misunderstandings, personality clashes, conflicting opinions, or different ideas about solutions.

To manage conflict effectively, it is essential to follow these steps:

❖ Acknowledge the Conflict: Denying that the conflict exists will not make it go away. Recognize that there is an issue and address it openly.

❖ Identify the Underlying Issue: To manage the conflict, it is important to identify the underlying issue. Doing so will ensure that substantial differences are genuinely being addressed instead of the superficial symptoms.

❖ Listen to the Other Party: Listen to the concerns of those involved in the conflict. Analyze what they are saying without becoming defensive and ask clarifying questions to gain a better understanding of their point of view.

❖ Collaborate to Generate Solutions: Collaborate to identify the possible solutions to the conflict. Work together to gain control of the situation and find potential solutions that satisfy all parties.

❖ Follow-Up: Follow up to ensure that the resolution was

effective. Create an action plan and identify the next steps to maintain ongoing communication to prevent the conflict from arising again.

## Real-life examples of Successful Collaboration

Collaboration is essential not only in business but in other fields. Let us take a look at some famous scientists and how they collaborated to achieve success.

### 1. Albert Einstein and Mileva Maric

In 1905 Albert Einstein and his wife Mileva Maric, a fellow physicist collaborated on a scientific paper exploring the behavior of electromagnetic radiation. The paper helped pave the way for Einstein's Theory of Special Relativity.

### 2. Marie and Pierre Curie

Married researchers, Marie, and Pierre Curie researched the radioactive elements Polonium and Radium in the late 19th century, leading to a greater understanding of radioactivity and winning them both Nobel Prizes in physics.

### 3. Steve Jobs and Steve Wozniak

The late Steve Jobs and his friend, Steve Wozniak, formed a company known as Apple. The two shared a love of technology, which drove them to develop some of the most significant technological advancements of our time.

## Conclusion

Collaborating with others is crucial in problem-solving. By following the strategies outlined above, individuals can maximize the benefits of collaboration, such as diverse thinking, shared knowledge, and skills, as well as minimizing the challenges. By communicating effectively and managing conflicts, you can form alliances that lead to groundbreaking other discoveries and innovative solutions.

# CHAPTER 13:
# LEADERSHIP

As a problem solver, you must also be a leader. In order to solve complex problems, you need to inspire and motivate your team to work collaboratively towards a common goal. Effective leadership is crucial to the success of any problem-solving effort.

**Importance of leadership in problem solving:**

Problem-solving is a team effort, and leaders play a crucial role in guiding the team to success. As a leader, you are responsible for defining the problem, setting goals, and formulating a strategy to achieve those goals. Effective leadership involves inspiring and motivating your team, creating a culture of innovation, and managing conflicts effectively.

**Different leadership styles:**

There are different leadership styles, and each of them has their own strengths and weaknesses. It is important to understand which style fits your personality and the situation at hand.

❖ Autocratic leadership style: In this style, the leader makes all decisions without seeking input from the team. This style can be effective in situations that require quick decision-making, but it can create resentment among team members.

❖ Democratic leadership style: In this style, the leader

involves the team in decision-making. This style leads to more satisfied team members but can be less effective in situations that require quick decisions.

❖　　　Transformational leadership style: Transformational leaders inspire and motivate their team members to work towards a common goal. This style is effective in situations that require innovation and creativity.

❖　　　Transactional leadership style: In this style, the leader sets clear goals and rewards team members who meet those goals. This style is effective in situations that need a clear chain of command.

## Techniques for motivating and inspiring others:

As a leader, you must motivate and inspire your team to work towards a common goal. Here are some techniques that can help you do that.

❖　　　Set clear goals: Clearly define the problem and set achievable goals that the team can work towards.

❖　　Communication: Communicate regularly with your team and share all relevant information about the project. This encourages an open and transparent culture within the team.

❖　　　Lead by example: Be a role model for your team by exhibiting hard work, perseverance, and a positive attitude.

❖　　　Recognition and reward: Recognize and reward team members for their contributions. This increases motivation and encourages team members to work harder.

## Importance of building trust and credibility:

Trust and credibility are essential ingredients for effective leadership. If team members do not trust or have confidence in their leader, their motivation and productivity will suffer.

Here are some ways to build trust and credibility with your team:

- ❖ Be honest and transparent: Communicate openly with your team and share all relevant information.

- ❖ Lead by example: Demonstrate your commitment to the project by working hard and contributing to the team effort.

- ❖ Listen to your team: Listen to the concerns and suggestions of your team members and be willing to incorporate their ideas into the project.

Real-life examples of effective leadership:

- ❖ Steve Jobs: Steve Jobs, the co-founder of Apple, is known as an effective leader who inspired his team to create innovative products. He was a transformational leader who set the vision for the company and inspired his team to work towards that vision.

- ❖ Mary Barra: Mary Barra is the CEO of General Motors and is known for her transparent and collaborative leadership style. She has successfully led the company through difficult times, and her leadership has inspired her team to work towards a common goal.

- ❖ Nelson Mandela: Nelson Mandela, the former president of South Africa, is known for his inspirational leadership style. He led a movement to end apartheid in the country, and his leadership inspired millions of people around the world.

## Conclusion:

In conclusion, effective leadership is essential to the success of any problem-solving effort. As a leader, you must inspire and motivate your team to work together towards a common goal. You must build trust and credibility with your team and create a culture of innovation and creativity. By doing so, you can lead your team to success and solve complex problems effectively.

# CHAPTER 14: CHANGE MANAGEMENT

Change is inevitable in any organization, whether it is driven by market factors, technological advancements, or business objectives. Change can bring growth, innovation, and progress, but it can also be disruptive, creating resistance, uncertainty, and fear. As a problem solver, it is important to understand the process of change management and the strategies for overcoming resistance, addressing obstacles, and achieving successful outcomes.

**The Process of Managing Change**

Change management involves a structured and disciplined approach to transitioning individuals, teams, and organizations from the current state to a desired future state. The process of change management typically involves these five steps:

❖　　Assess the current situation: Before embarking on any change initiative, assess the current state of the organization, including its strengths, weaknesses, opportunities, and threats. Identify the key stakeholders who will be impacted by the change and their concerns and expectations.

❖　Define the future state: Clearly define the desired future state of the organization, including the goals, objectives, and benefits of the change. Develop a clear vision, mission statement, and strategic plan that aligns with the organization's values and priorities.

❖ Plan and communicate: Develop a comprehensive change management plan that includes the key activities, timelines, milestones, and resources required to achieve the desired future state. Communicate the plan to all stakeholders who will be affected by the change and ensure that they have a clear understanding of the objectives, benefits, and risks of the change.

❖ Implement the change: Execute the change management plan, taking into account the potential obstacles and risks. Use a structured and systematic approach to manage the change process, monitor progress, and adjust course as needed.

❖ Measure and evaluate: Evaluate the effectiveness of the change management plan and assess the impact on the organization, the stakeholders, and the desired outcomes. Use a feedback loop to identify areas for improvement and develop strategies for continuous improvement.

## Importance of Planning and Communication

Effective change management requires careful planning and clear communication. Planning involves assessing the current situation, defining the desired future state, and developing a comprehensive plan of action that identifies the key activities, timelines, milestones, and resources required to achieve the desired outcomes. Communication involves informing, engaging, and empowering stakeholders at all levels of the organization, ensuring that they have a clear understanding of the objectives, benefits, and risks of the change.

Planning and communication are critical to successfully managing change for several reasons:

❖ Planning ensures that everyone is on the same page and working towards the same goals. Without a clear plan, stakeholders may have different expectations and priorities, leading to confusion and conflict.

❖ Communication builds trust and credibility, showing that the organization values and respects the concerns and opinions of its stakeholders. Effective communication also fosters a sense of ownership and commitment, encouraging stakeholders to take an active role in the change process.

❖ Planning and communication help to mitigate risks and avoid potential obstacles. By anticipating and addressing concerns and objections, the organization can minimize resistance and build momentum for the change.

**Overcoming Resistance to Change**

Resistance to change is a common and natural reaction to any significant organizational change. Resistance can take many forms, such as skepticism, anxiety, reluctance, and even hostility. As a problem solver, it is important to anticipate and understand the reasons for resistance and develop strategies for overcoming it.

Some common reasons for resistance to change include:

❖ Fear of the unknown: People may feel uneasy about the change and uncertain about their future roles and responsibilities.

❖ Loss of control: People may feel that the change is being imposed on them without their input or participation, leading to a loss of autonomy and control.

❖ Lack of trust: People may not trust the motives or abilities of the leaders spearheading the change, leading to skepticism and hostility.

❖ Overcoming resistance to change requires a proactive and empathetic approach that addresses the concerns and fears of the stakeholders. Here are some strategies to consider:

❖ Involve stakeholders in the change process: Give stakeholders a voice and a role in the change process, encouraging their participation and input.

❖ Communicate clearly and regularly: Keep stakeholders informed about the change process, addressing their concerns and objections, and providing feedback and updates.

❖ Build trust and credibility: Establish strong relationships with stakeholders and demonstrate your commitment to their well-being and success.

❖ Provide support and resources: Equip stakeholders with the tools, skills, and resources they need to adapt to the change and succeed in their new roles.

❖ Celebrate successes: Recognize and celebrate the achievements and milestones of the change process, acknowledging the contributions of all stakeholders.

## Identifying Potential Obstacles

Managing change can be challenging, and there are many potential obstacles that can derail even the best-laid plans. As a problem solver, it is important to anticipate and identify these obstacles and develop strategies for addressing them.

Some common obstacles to change management include:

❖ Lack of buy-in from key stakeholders: Resistance or reluctance from key stakeholders can hinder the success of the change initiative.

❖ Poor communication: Lack of clear and consistent

communication can lead to misunderstandings, confusion, and resistance.

❖    Inadequate planning: Failure to adequately plan the change initiative can result in delays, cost overruns, and insufficient resources.

❖    Overcoming these obstacles requires a proactive and strategic approach that addresses the root causes of the issues. Here are some strategies to consider:

❖    Build a coalition of support: Engage key stakeholders and build a coalition of supporters who can champion the change initiative and help to overcome resistance.

❖    Develop a comprehensive communication plan: Ensure that the communication plan is clear, comprehensive, and tailored to the needs of different stakeholder groups.

❖    Leverage expertise: Seek out and leverage the expertise of internal and external resources who can provide guidance and support for the change initiative.

❖    Adjust course as needed: Monitor progress and adjust course as needed to address issues and ensure that the change initiative is on track.

## Real-life examples of successful change management

One example of successful change management is the transformation of IBM from a struggling computer manufacturer to a technology and consulting industry leader. In the early 1990s, IBM faced significant challenges, including declining profitability, loss of market share, and inflexible organizational structure. In response, IBM implemented a comprehensive change management initiative that involved restructuring the company, refocusing on core businesses, and investing in new technologies and services. The change initiative involved extensive planning, communication, and stakeholder engagement, as well as a commitment to continuous improvement and innovation. The results of the change were significant and long-lasting, leading to increased profitability, market share, and customer satisfaction.

## Conclusion

Change management is a critical component of problem solving in any organization. Effective change management requires careful planning, clear communication, and strategies for overcoming resistance and addressing obstacles. By anticipating and understanding the potential challenges and developing proactive and empathetic approaches, problem solvers can successfully manage change and achieve desired outcomes.

# CHAPTER 15: INNOVATION

Innovation is often associated with groundbreaking new technologies, products, or services. However, innovation is more than that. Innovation is the process of creating something new or improving an existing product, service, or process to better meet the needs of customers or stakeholders. Innovation is essential for companies to stay competitive and relevant in today's ever-changing market. In this chapter, we will discuss the role of innovation in problem-solving, the approaches to fostering innovation, the importance of experimentation and risk-taking, and how to create a culture of innovation.

## The Role of Innovation in Problem Solving

Innovation is an essential component of problem-solving. In many cases, traditional problem-solving techniques do not provide feasible or effective solutions. In such scenarios, innovation plays a critical role in finding novel solutions to complex problems. Innovation-driven problem-solving approaches involve looking beyond what exists today and seeking entirely new solutions that can create a competitive advantage. Innovation-driven problem solving is characterized by experimentation, testing, and constant refining to find the most effective solution.

## Approaches to Fostering Innovation

Innovation is not a one-time activity that can be accomplished by following a set of established procedures. Fostering innovation involves creating an environment that encourages creative thinking and collaboration. Here are some approaches to fostering innovation in problem-solving.

❖ Encourage Creativity: Encouraging creativity means giving people the freedom to come up with new ideas and to experiment with different approaches. Innovation thrives in an environment that celebrates and encourages thinking outside the box.

❖ Promote Cross-Functional Collaboration: Cross-functional collaboration enables individuals from different departments to work together on a common problem. This approach helps in breaking down silos and encourages brainstorming of solutions from various perspectives.

❖ Provide Resources: Innovations require resources such as time, money, and expertise. Providing these resources can encourage experimentation and trial-and-error approaches to problem-solving.

❖ Recognize and Reward Innovative Ideas: Recognition and rewards incentivize innovation and motivate individuals to take the risk associated with experimentation. These rewards can be financial or non-financial but need to be meaningful and personalized to be effective.

## Encouraging Experimentation and Risk-Taking

Innovation-driven problem-solving approaches value experimentation and taking risks. Without taking risks, it is very unlikely that new and effective solutions will be discovered. The first step in encouraging experimentation and risk-taking is creating a safe environment for employees to take risks. Failure should be seen as a learning opportunity rather than as a reason for punishment. Encouraging experimentation helps build a culture of innovation where people continuously seek new and better solutions.

## Importance of Creating a Culture of Innovation

Creating a culture of innovation is essential for successful problem-solving. A culture of innovation prioritizes creative thinking, experimentation, and risk-taking, guides employee behavior, and is supported by the organization's structure and management. Organizations that promote innovation create an environment where employees feel comfortable sharing their ideas without fear of being judged and punished. Creating a culture of innovation requires a long-term investment in time and resources and a fundamental shift in organizational thinking toward being agile, adaptable, and willing to take risks.

## Real-life Examples of Successful Innovation

Innovation is an essential ingredient in creating a competitive advantage and driving business success. Successful organizations understand the value of innovation-driven problem-solving approaches and have a culture of innovation. Here are some real-life examples of successful innovation-driven problem-solving approaches.

❖    Apple: Apple is a well-known innovative company that has continuously produced innovative products. Apple is well-known for creating the iPhone, which revolutionized communication, and the iPad, which revolutionized mobile computing.

❖    Netflix: Netflix is an online streaming service that revolutionized the movie rental industry. They pioneered the concept of streaming and have since moved into producing original content, further cementing their position as an innovative force in the entertainment industry.

❖ Tesla: Tesla is a company that is using innovative technologies to transform the automobile industry. They are famous for their electric cars and recently introduced a new line of solar panels, which further underscores their commitment to innovation.

## Conclusion

Innovation is a critical component of problem-solving and is essential for organizations to stay competitive and relevant in today's market. Creating an environment that encourages creativity and experimentation and allows for risk-taking is crucial for fostering a culture of innovation. Success in innovation-driven problem-solving requires a long-term investment in time and resources. The creation of a culture of innovation can lead to breakthrough thinking and new solutions that create a competitive advantage for businesses.

# CHAPTER 16:
# CONTINUOUS
# IMPROVEMENT

Continuous improvement is an essential aspect of problem-solving. Many times, solutions may seem perfect in theory, but real-world implementation can highlight the loopholes. That is why continuous improvement is critical in ensuring we are not only solving problems but also finding ways to make the solutions better.

**Importance of continuous improvement**

Continuous improvement ensures your problem-solving process does not become stagnant. With an ever-changing business environment, it's impossible to assume solutions remain relevant. Customers' needs change, processes become outdated, and new technologies emerge. Without continuous improvement, your solutions may become obsolete.

Continuous improvement also helps organizations become more efficient and remain competitive. When you have a culture of continuous improvement, you will always be working towards being more efficient, reducing costs, and improving quality. This helps you stay ahead of the competition, meet customer needs, and boost shareholder value.

## Strategies for identifying areas for improvement

One of the best ways to identify areas of improvement is by seeking feedback. Feedback may come in various forms, such as customer feedback, employee feedback, and performance metrics. When collecting feedback, ensure you're asking the right questions that will help you identify problem areas.

Another way to identify areas for improvement is by monitoring trends. Keep up with industry publications and reports to identify emerging trends. This will help you anticipate changes that may require adjustments to your solutions.

Finally, continuous improvement requires a mindset of being open to feedback, accepting flaws, and seeking opportunities for improvement at all times. Encourage a culture of collaboration, wherein employees and stakeholders are comfortable voicing their suggestions and concerns.

## Implementing changes and measuring results

Once you have identified areas of improvement, the next step is to implement changes and measure results. It's essential to take a systematic approach to process change. Begin by communicating what changes will be made and why they're crucial.

Identify key performance indicators (KPIs) to track progress. KPIs will vary depending on the solution being improved, but it's crucial to align performance measures with the ultimate goal of the solution.

## Importance of feedback and iteration

Feedback is crucial in the continuous improvement process. Regularly seek feedback on the changes you've implemented to determine their effectiveness. Evaluate if the changes have achieved their intended goals, and if not, determine what adjustments need to be made. Iterate the process until the desired outcome is achieved.

## Real-life examples of successful continuous improvement

One excellent example of continuous improvement is Toyota's Kaizen philosophy. The company promotes a culture of continuous improvement, wherein every employee is encouraged to identify potential improvements in their work processes. The company has reaped the benefits of Kaizen, including increased efficiency, improved quality, and reduced costs.

Another example is Amazon's approach to innovation. Every year, Amazon CEO Jeff Bezos mandates that all departments eliminate non-essential expenses and reinvest the savings in new initiatives. By continuously iterating and improving on their processes, Amazon has become one of the most innovative and customer-centric companies in the world.

## Conclusion

Continuous improvement is crucial for staying competitive, meeting customer needs, and achieving business goals. It requires a mindset of constant reflection, open communication, and willingness to adapt to change. Continuous improvement helps organizations remain agile, adaptable, and relevant in an ever-changing business environment. To achieve successful continuous improvement, organizations must seek feedback, implement changes systematically, measure results, iterate, and repeat the process.

# CHAPTER 17:
# PROBLEM SOLVING IN
# DIFFERENT CONTEXTS

Problem solving is an essential skill that can benefit individuals in various fields, from business to healthcare to education to public service. However, different industries pose unique challenges that require specific approaches to problem solving. In this chapter, we will explore how problem solving can be applied in different contexts and the common challenges in each of these areas, along with real-life examples of successful problem solving.

## Business

Businesses of any size face complex problems such as declining sales, customer dissatisfaction, or employee turnover. Problem-solving in the business context requires a strategic perspective and an ability to prioritize tasks. The following are some of the common challenges faced in this area:

❖ Limited Resources: Businesses have limited resources for problem-solving, and, therefore, it is vital to identify the most critical problems to solve. This can be done by taking stock of the most significant challenges that are urgent and have the most significant impact on the business.

❖ Innovation: Business problems require creative solutions as organizations seek to remain competitive and create unique value propositions for their customers. Therefore, problem solvers must think outside the box and innovate.

❖ Speed: The fast-moving pace of the business world demands swift action in the face of urgent problems. Problem solvers must act quickly and decisively.

## Healthcare

The healthcare industry is complex and multifaceted. With the development of new technologies, problem-solving has become more challenging in this field. Some of the common challenges faced in this area include:

❖ Technical complexity: Healthcare problems are often highly technical and require a deep understanding of biological, physical, and chemical processes. Therefore, healthcare providers must have a deep understanding of medical science to solve problems.

❖ Regulations: Healthcare is a heavily regulated industry, and each nation has different laws that govern patient care, innovation, and reimbursement. Problem solvers need an understanding of the legal landscape to find the right solutions.

❖ Patient-centric approach: Central to healthcare is a focus on patient care. Solving healthcare problems requires a focus on improving patient care while balancing other considerations such as cost, access, and quality.

## Education

Education faces several challenges and complexities today, such as budget cuts, limited resources, and the need to remain relevant and innovative constantly. Effective problem-solving in education should involve stakeholders and use data-driven approaches. Some of the common challenges that education faces include:

❖ Limited Resources: Schools and higher education institutions operate on tight budgets. Therefore, problem solvers must focus on identifying creative solutions that can be implemented using limited resources.

❖ Changing landscape: Education is continually changing, and this requires educators to adapt and be innovative in the solutions they create. Problem solvers need to understand the latest in technology, teaching methods, and student needs to be effective in addressing problems in education.

❖ Stakeholder involvement: Education problems are best solved by including all stakeholders, such as educators, parents, students, government, and community. Problem solvers must build bridges among stakeholders to identify comprehensive solutions.

## Public Service

The public service sector includes government agencies, non-profit organizations, and social enterprises, all of which have a specific set of challenges. For problem solvers in this industry, a focus on the public good is paramount. Some of the common challenges faced in this area include:

❖ Complexity: Public sector problems might involve several government departments, public organizations, and private firms. Therefore, problem solvers should have a holistic approach that considers the needs of different stakeholders.

❖ Policies and Regulations: Public service organizations operate within established policies and regulations, and problem solvers must be able to navigate them effectively.

❖ Accountability and transparency: Public service organizations must be accountable to the public they serve. Solving problems in this sector requires a transparent and open approach.

## Real-life Examples of Successful Problem-Solving

One of the most famous examples of problem-solving is NASA's Apollo program, which successfully put a man on the moon in 1969. The program used a collaborative approach that integrated various organizations and experts in technology, science, and engineering. Problem-solving challenges, such as developing an efficient and lightweight spacecraft, required creative thinking from different fields and solved major technical issues such as lunar landing, return, and Earth re-entry. Another example is Tesla's electric car technology that emphasizes the importance of a human-centric approach and innovation that made electric cars become a profitable business. The company had to overcome resistance from incumbent carmakers, lack of charging infrastructure, and skepticism about electric cars' performance, but Tesla was able to solve these problems and create a unique offering in the market.

## Conclusion

Problem-solving is an essential skill that can be applied in different contexts and industries. However, each industry may require unique approaches to problem-solving and has unique challenges to overcome. Successful problem-solving in any industry requires applying the problem-solving process by identifying the key problem, setting a strategic approach, gathering relevant data, generating creative ideas, evaluating, and selecting the best-fit solutions, and monitoring the implementation progress. Ultimately, one can develop effective problem-solving by continually improving their skills, seeking feedback, reflecting on their experiences and feedback, and iterating as necessary.

# CHAPTER 18:
# PROBLEM SOLVING
# IN THE DIGITAL AGE

In today's world, technology is advancing at a rapid pace, creating new opportunities and challenges for problem solving. Digital problem solving is becoming increasingly important, as many traditional problems are now being solved through digital means. In this chapter, we'll explore the impact of technology on problem solving, the tools and resources available for digital problem solving, and real-life examples of successful digital problem solving.

## The Impact of Technology on Problem Solving

Digital technology has enabled us to tackle problems in new and innovative ways. For example, big data analytics, machine learning, and artificial intelligence are all technologies that have revolutionized how we approach problem solving. These tools allow us to process and analyze large amounts of data quickly and efficiently, enabling us to identify patterns and trends that would be difficult to spot manually.

Another advantage of technology is that it allows us to collaborate with others remotely. Tools such as video conferencing and instant messaging make it easier for teams to work together across different locations and time zones. This can be particularly helpful when working on complex problems that require input from a variety of experts.

The downside of technology is that it can also create new problems. For example, the Internet has made it easier for cybercriminals to launch attacks on businesses and individuals, threatening the security of our data and systems. Similarly, social media has created new challenges when it comes to managing reputational risk and dealing with online trolls.

## Opportunities and Challenges of Digital Problem Solving

One of the main opportunities presented by digital problem solving is the ability to automate routine tasks, freeing up time for more strategic thinking. For example, artificial intelligence can be used to analyze financial data and identify trends, allowing financial analysts to focus on making strategic decisions rather than spending time on manual data entry.

Another opportunity is the ability to leverage social media to gather feedback from customers and stakeholders. Social listening tools can be used to monitor what people are saying about a company or product online, providing valuable insights that can be used to inform decisions.

However, digital problem solving also presents challenges. One challenge is the need to constantly adapt to new technologies as they emerge. As soon as we become proficient in one tool or platform, a new one comes along that requires us to learn new skills.

Another challenge is the potential for information overload. With so much data available online, it can be difficult to filter out the noise and focus on what's important. This is where analytical and critical thinking skills become particularly important, as we need to be able to identify the key insights and trends that will inform our decisions.

## Tools and Resources for Digital Problem Solving

There are a variety of tools and resources available for digital problem solving. Here are a few examples:

❖ Data visualization tools: These tools allow us to turn complex data sets into easy-to-understand visualizations such as charts, graphs, and heat maps. This can be particularly helpful when we're trying to identify patterns and trends.

❖ Collaboration platforms: Tools such as Slack and Teams make it easier for teams to work together across different locations and time zones. They provide a centralized location for sharing files, communicating, and tracking progress.

❖ Social listening tools: These tools allow us to monitor what people are saying about a company or product online. This can be helpful in identifying trends, gathering feedback, and managing reputational risk.

❖ Big data analytics tools: These tools allow us to analyze large amounts of data quickly and efficiently, identifying patterns and trends that would be difficult to spot manually.

❖ Project management tools: Tools such as Trello and Asana can be helpful in managing complex projects, providing a visual representation of tasks and deadlines.

## Real-Life Examples of Successful Digital Problem Solving

Here are a few examples of successful digital problem solving in action:

❖ IBM's Watson: IBM's Watson is an artificial intelligence platform that has been used to solve a variety of complex problems, from diagnosing diseases to predicting weather patterns. Watson's ability to analyze large amounts of data quickly and efficiently has made it a valuable tool in many industries.

❖ Airbnb: Airbnb uses a variety of digital tools to solve problems related to managing a large number of hosts and guests across the world. For example, its "smart pricing" algorithm uses machine learning to adjust prices based on supply and demand, ensuring that hosts get the best price for their property.

❖ Netflix: Netflix uses big data analytics to recommend shows and movies to its users based on their viewing history. Its algorithms analyze everything from which shows a user has watched to how long they've watched each episode, allowing it to make personalized recommendations that keep users engaged.

## Conclusion

Digital technology has revolutionized the way we approach problem solving, offering new opportunities, and presenting new challenges. To be successful in the digital age, it's important to stay up-to-date with the latest tools and technologies, while also developing strong analytical, critical thinking, and communication skills. With the right mindset and tools, anyone can be successful in solving problems in the digital age.

# CHAPTER 19: ETHICS AND PROBLEM SOLVING

As we delve deeper into the art of problem solving, it is essential to consider the ethical implications that may arise during the process. Ethics play a vital role in problem-solving skills as it helps in considering different perspectives and analyzing the impact of our decisions on those affected by it. Ethical decision-making is not an option but a necessity to build trust, foster goodwill and uphold your reputation. In this chapter, we will discuss the importance of ethics in problem-solving, identifying potential ethical dilemmas, approaches to ethical decision-making, and ethical leadership in problem-solving.

**Importance of ethical considerations in problem-solving:**

Problem solving is a complex process that involves multiple variables, and decisions taken in haste without considering the ethical implications can cause significant impacts on individuals and communities. Ethics help us to recognize our values and beliefs, identify what is right or wrong, and ensure that our decisions are justifiable and defendable. Therefore, it is crucial to consider ethical aspects like fairness, accountability, respect, dignity, and responsibility while making decisions.

**Identifying potential ethical dilemmas:**

Ethical dilemmas can arise at any stage of problem-solving, from identifying the problem to implementing the solutions. It may involve conflicting values, ethical principles, moral obligations, and societal norms. For example, balancing the need for a job against environmental protection, maximizing profits against employee welfare, and equal distribution of resources against cost minimization. Therefore, it is imperative to recognize these potential ethical dilemmas early on, assess the possible consequences and strive to find a balance that upholds moral standards while solving the problem.

**Approaches to ethical decision making:**

Making ethical decisions is not an easy task, as it involves trade-offs between various interests of stakeholders. However, Various models and approaches can help us to make informed, reasoned, and defendable decisions that uphold ethical principles and values. Some of these approaches are:

- ❖ Utilitarian approach: In this approach, the decision taken is based on maximizing the overall utility or happiness of society or the majority of stakeholders.

- ❖ Deontological approach: In this approach, the decision taken is based on universal moral principles or duties without considering consequences or outcomes.

- ❖ Virtue Approach: In this approach, the decision taken is based on cultivating virtues or character traits like honesty, integrity, and compassion.

- ❖ Justice Approach: In this approach, the decision taken is based on fairness and equality for all stakeholders, regardless of their position or status.

**Ethical leadership in problem-solving:**

Leaders play a crucial role in promoting ethical problem-solving. As a leader, one should lead by example, establish a culture of ethics, act with integrity, and hold oneself accountable for one's decisions and actions. Every leader must foster an environment that promotes transparency, encourages open dialogue, and welcomes diverse perspectives that can contribute to robust ethical decision-making.

## Real-life examples of ethical problem-solving:

The recent global pandemic has tested problem-solving skills and ethical decision-making like never before. Governments and organizations have been facing ethical dilemmas over the allocation of resources, prioritizing safety, and managing the economy. One such example is the controversy over making vaccines available to the rich rather than prioritizing frontline workers, older adults, and vulnerable populations.

In conclusion, ethical considerations are essential in problem-solving as it helps in identifying potential ethical dilemmas, approaches to ethical decision-making, and ethical leadership. While solving a problem, it is vital to assess the implications of the decision on stakeholders, the environment, and society. As a problem solver, one must strive to uphold moral and ethical standards while tackling complex issues.

# CHAPTER 20: CONCLUSION AND APPLICATION

Throughout this book, we have explored different aspects of problem-solving and how it is relevant to various areas of life, such as professional development, personal growth, and societal change. We have examined different techniques and skills that can help us to approach problems in a structured and systematic way, such as understanding the problem, brainstorming solutions, evaluating them, implementing them, reflecting on the process, and continuously improving.

As we conclude this book, it is important to take a moment to reflect on what we have learned and how we can apply it to our lives. The art of problem-solving is not just a theoretical concept; it is a skill that we can cultivate through practice and continuous learning. By applying problem-solving skills, we can approach challenges in a more effective and efficient manner, making more informed decisions and taking more calculated risks.

One of the key takeaways from this book is the importance of perseverance. Problem-solving is not always easy; in fact, it can be quite challenging and frustrating at times. However, by staying committed to the process and being persistent in seeking solutions, we can overcome even the most complex problems.

Another important theme that runs throughout this book is the significance of collaboration. Problem-solving is often a team effort, and the ability to work effectively with others is essential for achieving success. By leveraging the strengths of different individuals, we can achieve more than we can on our own.

Furthermore, ethical considerations are an essential aspect of problem-solving. As we apply our skills in different contexts, we must remain aware of ethical implications and act with integrity and responsibility.

To apply problem-solving skills in our lives, we can start by identifying areas where we would like to make improvements. Whether it is a personal or professional challenge, we can begin by breaking it down into smaller, more manageable components and applying the techniques outlined in this book. By doing so, we can develop solutions that are feasible, effective, and ethical.

In addition, we can cultivate a habit of continuous learning and improvement. By remaining open to new perspectives and approaches, we can stay up-to-date with the latest developments in our respective fields and be better equipped to tackle future challenges.

Ultimately, by mastering the art of problem-solving, we can become more efficient, effective, and adaptable individuals, capable of achieving success in various areas of life. We hope that this book has helped to equip you with the tools and skills necessary to become a successful problem solver and that you will continue to apply these skills to your personal and professional life.

Real-life examples of how readers have used problem-solving skills in their personal and professional lives:

❖ Sarah, a small business owner, used problem-solving skills to identify and overcome challenges in her business, such as optimizing processes, improving communication with customers, and navigating changes in the market.

❖ John, a teacher, applied problem-solving skills when designing lesson plans, addressing student needs, and learning styles, and collaborating with other educators to improve curriculum and instruction.

❖ Carla, a community activist, used problem-solving skills to identify and address social and environmental issues in her community, such as advocating for better transportation options, promoting sustainability practices, and empowering marginalized groups.

❖ Mike, a software developer, applied problem-solving skills to develop innovative solutions for clients, troubleshoot technical issues, and stay up-to-date with new developments in the industry.

❖ Tina, a healthcare professional, used problem-solving skills to improve patient outcomes, streamline procedures, and address ethical considerations in healthcare.

These are just a few examples of how problem-solving skills can be applied in different contexts. By being intentional about developing and applying these skills, we can become more effective problem solvers and make a positive impact in the world around us.

## Final Thoughts

Mastering the art of problem solving is not just about finding solutions to immediate problems; it is a lifelong skill that can transform your personal and professional life. By developing an analytical mindset, cultivating creativity, and embracing persistence, we can tackle any challenge that comes our way with confidence and clarity.

Remember, there is no one-size-fits-all approach to problem-solving. What works for one person may not work for another.

The key is to constantly learn from your experiences, reflect on what worked and what didn't, and adjust accordingly.

I hope this book has provided you with valuable insights into the art of problem-solving. However, reading alone won't make you a master problem solver; practice will. So go out there and apply these principles in your daily life, whether it's at work or in your personal relationships.

In the end, I believe that by mastering the art of problem-solving, we can create a more fulfilling life for ourselves and those around us. We can overcome challenges with grace and resilience and become better versions of ourselves along the way.

# ABOUT THE AUTHOR

## Ray Goodwin

Ray Goodwin, is the author behind this series of captivating books on Business Development and self improvement, and has left an indelible mark on the field. He was born and raised in the bustling city of London, where he developed a strong work ethic and an insatiable curiosity about the inner workings of successful businesses. Throughout his illustrious career, Ray leveraged his extensive knowledge and experience to help numerous companies flourish and prosper.

His keen insights and innovative strategies has earned him recognition, driving him to share his expertise with others. Ray believes in the power of sharing knowledge to elevate businesses and empower aspiring entrepreneurs.

Ray's dedication to his craft is evident in the numerous books he has authored on business development and self improvement. His writing style seamlessly blends practical advice, thought-provoking concepts, and real-life case studies, making his books invaluable resources for business professionals and novices alike. His ability to distill complex concepts into accessible language has greatly impacted the lives and careers of countless individuals.

Now retired from the corporate world, Ray and his beloved wife have settled in the idyllic English countryside. Surrounded by the beauty of nature, Ray finds inspiration for his writing and indulges in his hobbies.

Ray Goodwin's books continue to serve as enduring guides for those seeking success in the business world. With a wealth of experience and a deep understanding of the inner workings of businesses, Ray's work remains a testament to his passion for sharing knowledge and helping others flourish.